Valley Lemons

Karina Flores

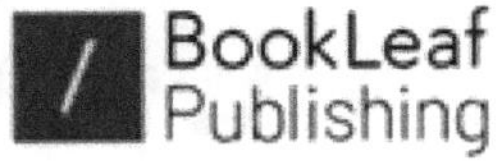

Presentation by *BookLeaf Publishing*

Web: www.bookleafpub.com

E-mail: info@bookleafpub.com

ISBN: 9789357213264

First edition 2023

Valley Lemon

My roots have been planted on the same soil as
my ancestors,
their wisdom fertilizes my mind with ancient
truths
This same soil is known to bear bountiful
citruses despite its seemingly inhospitable
climate
It is my home,
A once thought to be barren land,
bountiful,
Once thought to amount to nothing,
fruitful and desired
Once seemingly a burden,
now recognized for its wealth and what it has to
offer
And isn't that always the way?
Here, on this same soil, grows the Valley Lemon
And, like the Valley Lemon
I should be bitter, but I am anything but
Instead, like the Valley Lemon,
I am sweet
I am tender
I have thin skin, prone to bruising
overly sensitive,
feels too much

but
I know that my roots are deep
And will keep me grounded

Page Turner

There's a story here
But are you the right person to hear it?

Would you listen willingly?
Or shy away

Like a cadaver in autopsy,
Its story written within the map of its nerves and
muscles
Cause of death?
Unknown.

Would you open your eyes, ears, hearts?
Absorb, or abstain
The story is ours
If you make it ours
If you allow yourself
To turn the page

Courage

Let it
Let it embolden you
Surround you
Scare the living shit out of you
Break you
Awaken you

Let it be worthy
Let it be love

Signs

I waited
For the world to speak to me
Through me
For me

And it has come to my attention that
Signs don't work that way
They are only there because they are willed to be
there
And if you seek, you shall find

On Thought

I've had lots of thoughts recently
Amid the torrent-ridden chaos
Or all too familiar deafening silence that ensues
when one sits with their own mind
Minds can be quite an entity all their own
They conjure up such fanciful thoughts,
thoughts that wouldn't have otherwise been
thought of
If it were not for daydreams or night terrors
It is precisely this type of lucid, free-forming,
star dripped galaxy of ideas
that flows and penetrates through the
membranes of my cerebral cortex that reminds
me
of the duplicity of human nature
Reminds me that evil is one twisted decision
away,
As is whimsy
As is romance
Thought, with intention, can be quite a powerful
weapon
Put in the right hands with those who know how
to wield it

Quiet Girl

The casual observer
The know-it-all
She doesn't speak to anyone
Dares not say a word, though she is fully aware
of the happenings around her
Knows the misconceptions
Knows that her silence is misinterpreted as
weakness
When really it's just a matter of not wanting to
engage
Not wanting to waste her energy on things that
no longer serve her
She wants real,
She wants genuine,
Her mind, a universe with its own gravitational
pull
Only the lucky ones will be able to orbit

Public Gathering

Congregate,
A sea of electricity
Waves which ebb and flow
Waters filled with thoughts
Each mind a universe
Interconnected
Worlds abound
Worlds.
Bound.
Formed in either inhibitions or exhibitions
Public displays or private existence
Makes no difference
      the energy remains
in constant flux

Sleep Paralysis

Jolt.

The mind,
Awake.
The body,
lies still, as if the muscles have atrophied.

someone has pulled the plug on the mind from
its host
The electric currents have gone haywire,
messages are not being received
and are depriving the body of conciousness,

the mind flops, a helpless fish out of water,

trapped
in
limbo

The mind desperately pleas, "Move, please
move."

There is a bright, ominous glow in the corner of
the room
It comes claiming a debt

It stalks, hunter and prey

Another jolt.

The mind once again pleads, "Turn, lift a finger.
Move."
Pleas for the body to listen to the mind once
more
Pleas for the mind to connect with the body once
more

The darkness closes in, and feels like death has
come

Until there is the slightest of movements
And a reminder of how breathing works

Blue Light Abyss

Wake.
scroll.
Groan.
scroll.

Pain.
Sadness.
Apathy.

Wake.

Scroll.

-tethered-

Scroll.

can't
look
away

Wake up, or
Fall victim to willful blindness
A clear image on full display, 4K resolution with
pixilated dread

It's ugly out there
Hard, out there. Scary, out there.
Uncertain, out there.

Lay.
  Scroll.
    Turn.
      Scroll.

A Writer's Lament

Words are absolutely failing me
My brain, a slotted spoon
Thoughts that refuse to solidify
Reduce themselves to a liquified goop that
would sooner drip into a garbage disposal
than be given life
And isn't that a lovely irony?

They sense my desperation, don't they?
Those clever, conniving words

No Oxford dictionary
No Webster's definition can explain
Why something so
Malleable
　Effervescent
　　Exquisite
　　　So

　　　　　So

　　　　　　So

Oh, come on now you damned words,
Horrid things,
Am I not a worthy enough host for you to flow
through me and take life?

That's it, isn't it?

My desperation betrays me,
and they sense it

Faulty Optimism

Hello?
Yes, I'm calling in regard to optimism
Yes, I know, sunny disposition, YOLO, look on
the bright side and all that, but
No, I
…just listen
I think mine is faulty
See cause there's this thick, dark, looming cloud
of, um, I think they call it pessimism?

Yes, pessimism
Uh-huh, factory reset?
I've tried.
The pessimism doesn't go away

Nope, tried that too. Doesn't go away
It's just hanging over me,
Yes, I hear what you're saying but I don't think
you're listening to me
It's not working, my optimism is not working
No, see, because I keep having this thing, what
do they call it? Um, existential dread?
I keep thinking that it's all for not, and that this
living thing is hard

And that we're all doomed and that it's all
pointless and that we really shouldn't lie to
ourselves
What was that? What?
Oh no, please don't put me on hold again
Wait, wait
Hello?

A Picture of Destiny

Destiny provides no heralds, Wilde once said
She is too wise or too cruel
And whatever her reason
Life is too precious
Too magical
To stay fixated on consequence
For if you knew you would fail, you would not
try
And if success was imminently on the horizon,
The journey would be meaningless

Nature Treasure Trove

Within the troves of nature
Every tree,
Bird,
Trail,
Winding path,
Fallen leaf with changing colors,
Every tranquil moment,
A treasure

Dew

Morning
The day's first light reveals twining vines knit together
forming, extending, eagerly absorbing the air's moisture

Dripping dew drops
Radiating from the glow of sunrise

This is the veil of new possibility
lifting itself, calling

Luna and Mar

Luna, she glows in the night sky. Her radiance is iridescent as it hits the surface of the shore. The seam where the sand first meets the water is always the warmest and where Mar feels her presence strongest. Luna pulls Mar, she attempts to bring him close to her like a lover that lingers for a warm embrace. Mar has attempted many times to reach his Luna, his waves climb high as mountains in attempts to pierce through the night sky.

Try as he might, he can never reach her. Though Mar is vast, Luna is always beyond his reach. I dip my toes in the shore as I watch this exchange. Knowing full well that their love is of the star-crossed kind. But their persistence, their longing. It is the kind of love that you know is beautiful from afar but tragic up close. Luna and Mar, moon, and ocean. In the stitching of the world, they were never meant to be on the same cloth.

Honey

We work diligently for our Queen
Her kingdom, our haven
Our home,
A sacred, sanctified
Holy Place
We are honored to create this sweet nectar
This golden, precious delicacy
All for her
All for honor
We worship her
We

Wait,
…. What is that?

What is this? What is happening?

The fumes, the fumes
No, not again
They come again, the standing ones
They wreak havoc

Mystified,
We are helpless to their tactics
Forced to retreat, to leave behind all we know

Again, and again, and again, and again

Was once not enough?
Don't know if there is enough strength to start
anew
That may have been the last of it
The last of our Honey

Thieves of the
World

They tried to oppress us
To tell us what's good
To tell us what to believe
To hold us hostage on our own land
Sell us on the fallacy that we are not the true
dwellers

While they hijacked our home,
we always knew the truth

And the thieves of the world will have their
reckoning
Because nothing ever goes unseen

Child

My wounded child never leaves me
She stays within the recesses of my mind,
Reminds me every now and again of that
Time
My mother told me she hated me
Place
Without power, without heat on a cold Christmas
day

Memories, which hurt me
remind me that my spirit was once broken

I kneel down to meet her,
Say to the young, wounded child,
"Do not fear, we are on the mend."

Mortality

"The beauty of love is that, like water, it has no shape. But it is the most powerful element in the world, and it breaks through rock and steel. And it's powerful because it's malleable and gentle."
-Guillermo Del Toro

Grief and love
Two of the strongest emotions that I have ever witnessed
I've seen the eyes of grief and love
The resemblance is striking
The body lets out a heavy sigh, allowing it to sink and become weightless all at the same time
Revealing a simultaneous release and refrain
A sort of hopelessness that can only be caught at the first sight of vulnerability
For at that moment, there are no expectations
But still, so many
We've been told the rules of living
And yet, we dare to ask for forever
        that sheer dissonance
that gumption and entitlement of the human spirit
It is that innate ability to feel,

be enveloped, possessed, awakened, broken, revived
feelings beyond our own understanding
Reminding us once more what it means to be alive

Consejo (Advice)

I miss her
We had a language barrier
And you can blame that on an education system
that hammered in the English language
Leaving Spanish by the wayside

I miss her, my Abuela
I miss her, though we could barely communicate

I spoke broken Spanish
Told her that I was doing okay in school
That I was doing okay at work
Todo va bien, I'd repeat over and over
Would recycle the same words hoping that
they'd find new meaning

But despite the barrier
There was no wall between us
She was warm, inviting

Made sure to feed us, though we'd sometimes
arrive with no appetite
But you ate because she cooked it with amor,
and you better respect that

We'd spend all afternoon in her home, watching
late night Spanish variety tv like Sábado Gigante
While ama and her discussed the latest gossip of
our family
I wish I could have spoken to her
Learn about our story
And tell you about it, really tell you
Because I just know her story was fascinating
But she left,
before I could find the words
My piece of advice?
Find the words

Thin Skin

When I was a child,
I tested my skin,
put my fingers directly atop a steaming iron
Mirroring my mother, who practiced this
technique to check its heat
My mistake, I didn't hover above
I placed my delicate fingers directly onto the
iron
Felt my flesh sting,
Yelped, cried for mama to come into the room
"I wanted to help, mama"
She held my tiny hand into hers,
"Sana, sana," she cooed to me
My skin bubbled, and she ran for an ointment
I watched my skin as it slowly ballooned
Silent, brave little tears were welling in my
behind my eyes,
but I dare not cry
No, I want to be strong,
like mama
She came, rubbed the ointment, kissed my
forehead
"It will be okay," she said to me, "it will heal in
time"

When I was a teenager,
My Dad would call attention to himself by way
of incoherent yelling, one of the many
symptoms
Brought on by a disease known as alcoholism
Mom would try to reason with him, but there
was no reasoning with a man who had no control
And he would lose his control, quite often
He would yell at her
Quite often
Mama is so strong, I would think to myself, she
never cries

One day I searched for her after one of Dad's
episodes,
I found her, she was sitting alone in the family
car
She was crying,
I hid as she climbed out of the car
She didn't want me to see

But I wanted to tell her
Mama, it's okay to have thin skin
It's okay to feel

Remember what you told me?
It will be okay, it will heal in time

9 789357 213264